Fun Time Sweaters

What was her favorite thing about the matinee?

She got to share popcorn with her best friend. And she decided that fruit punch was way better than lemon-lime soda. Of course, the movie was really funny! But her favorite thing was gettir wear her new sweater, the soft one you knit for her.

With original details like scallops, twisted trim, stripes, tie cl and ruffles, all five of these fresh designs are perfect to wear to the movies, the park, the pizza parlor—anywhere a girl can have fun!

LEISURE ARTS, INC.
Little Rock, Arkansas

Scalloped Cardigan

INTERMEDIATE

Size	Finished Chest Measurement	
2	23"	(58.5 cm)
4	25"	(63.5 cm)
6	27"	(68.5 cm)
8	$28^1/_2$"	(72.5 cm)
10	$31^1/_2$"	(80 cm)

Size Note: Instructions are written with sizes 2 and 4 in the first set of braces { } and sizes 6, 8, and 10 in the second set of braces. Instructions will be easier to read if you circle all the numbers pertaining to your size. If only one number is given, it applies to all sizes.

MATERIALS

Light Weight Yarn (LIGHT 3)
[$1^3/_4$ ounces, 114 yards
(50 grams, 104 meters) per skein]:
{4-4}{5-7-7} skeins
24" (61 cm) Circular needle, size 6 (4 mm) **or** size needed for gauge
Straight knitting needles, size 6 (4 mm)
Stitch holders - 2
$^1/_4$" (7 mm) Buttons - {5-6}{6-7-7}
Point protectors - 2
Yarn needle

GAUGE: In pattern,
18 sts and 24 rows = 4" (10 cm)

Body is worked in one piece to armholes.

SCALLOPED EDGING

Scallops are worked individually, then joined to begin the Body.

FIRST SCALLOP

With circular needle, cast on {4-8}{8-12-12} sts.

Rows 1-6: (P2, K2) across.

Note: Loop a short piece of yarn around any stitch to mark Row 6 as **right** side.

Cut yarn; leave Scallop on needle.

SECOND SCALLOP

With **right** side of previous Scallop(s) facing and on right end of circular needle, cast on {4-8}{8-12-12} sts to same end of needle.

Rows 1-6: (K2, P2) across.

Note: Mark Row 6 as **right** side.

Cut yarn; leave Scallop on needle.

THIRD SCALLOP

With **right** side of previous Scallops facing and on right end of circular needle, cast on {4-8}{8-12-12} sts to same end of needle.

Rows 1-6: (P2, K2) across.

Note: Mark Row 6 as **right** side.

Cut yarn; leave Scallop on needle.

REMAINING SCALLOPS

Repeat Second and Third Scallops, {7-4}{4-3-3} times; then repeat Second Scallop, {0-0}{1-0-1} time(s) **more** *(see Zeros, page 29)*; at end of last Scallop, do **not** cut yarn: {17-11}{12-9-10} Scallops.

BODY

SIZES 2, 4, AND 8 ONLY

Joining Row: Add on 2 sts *(Figs. 5a & b, page 30)*, K2, (P2, K2) across Scallop, **turn**, add on 2 sts, ★ **turn**, (K2, P2) across Scallop, **turn**, add on 2 sts, **turn**, (P2, K2) across Scallop, **turn**, add on 2 sts; repeat from ★ across: {104-112}{128} sts.

SIZES 6 AND 10 ONLY

Joining Row: Add on 2 sts *(Figs. 5a & b, page 30)*, P2, (K2, P2) across Scallop; **turn**, add on 2 sts, **turn**, (P2, K2) across Scallop, **turn**, add on 2 sts, ★ **turn**, (K2, P2) across Scallop, **turn**, add on 2 sts, **turn**, (P2, K2) across Scallop, **turn**, add on 2 sts; repeat from ★ across: {122-142} sts.

ALL SIZES

Row 1 (Right side)**:** (K2, P2) across to last {0-0}{2-0-2} sts, K{0-0}{2-0-2}.

Row 2: P{0-0}{2-0-2}, (K2, P2) across.

Repeat Rows 1 and 2 for pattern until Body measures approximately {7$^1/_2$-9}{9$^1/_2$-10-10}"/{19-23}{24-25.5-25.5} cm from cast on edge of Scallops, ending by working Row 2.

Maintain established pattern throughout.

Dividing Row: Work across {23-24}{24-26-29} sts (Right Front), bind off next {4-6}{10-10-10} sts, work across next {49-51}{53-55-63} sts (Back), bind off next {4-6}{10-10-10} sts, work across remaining {22-23}{23-25-28} sts (Left Front).

Instructions continued on page 4.

LEFT FRONT

Row 1: With empty straight needle, work across Left Front sts; leave remaining sts on circular needle and place point protectors on ends: {23-24}{24-26-29} sts.

Work even on straight needles until Left Front measures approximately {10-12}{12¾-13½-14}"/{25.5-30.5}{32.5-34.5-35.5} cm from cast on edge of Scallops, ending by working a **right** side row.

NECK SHAPING

Row 1: Bind off {6-7}{7-8-8} sts, work across: {17-17}{17-18-21} sts.

Row 2 (Decrease row)**:** Work across to last 2 sts, K2 tog *(Fig. 7, page 30)*: {16-16}{16-17-20} sts.

Row 3: Work across.

Repeat Rows 2 and 3, {2-2}{2-3-3} times: {14-14}{14-14-17} sts.

Work even until Left Front measures approximately {12½-14½}{15½-16½-17}"/{32-37}{39.5-42-43} cm from cast on edge of Scallops, ending by working a **wrong** side row.

Cut yarn leaving a long end for 3-Needle Bind Off. Slip remaining {14-14}{14-14-17} sts onto st holder.

RIGHT FRONT

With **wrong** side facing, slip Right Front sts onto empty straight needle, leave remaining sts on circular needle and replace point protectors on ends: {23-24}{24-26-29} sts.

Work even on straight needles until Right Front measures same as Left Front to Neck Shaping, ending by working a **wrong** side row.

NECK SHAPING

Row 1: Bind off {6-7}{7-8-8} sts, work across: {17-17}{17-18-21} sts.

Row 2: Work across.

Row 3 (Decrease row)**:** SSK *(Figs. 8a-c, page 30)*, work across: {16-16}{16-17-20} sts.

Repeat Rows 2 and 3, {2-2}{2-3-3} time(s): {14-14}{14-14-17} sts.

Work even until Right Front measures same as Left Front, ending by working a **right** side row.

Cut yarn leaving a long end for 3-Needle Bind Off. Slip remaining {14-14}{14-14-17} sts onto st holder.

BACK

With circular needle, work even until Back measures same as Fronts, ending by working a **right** side row.

Leave sts on circular needle. Do **not** cut yarn.

SHOULDER JOINING

Slip sts from Left Front stitch holder onto straight needle. Using 3-Needle Bind Off *(Fig. 10, page 31)*, join first {14-14}{14-14-17} sts of Back to Left Front.

Slip sts from Right Front st holder onto straight needle. Using 3-Needle Bind Off, join last {14-14}{14-14-17} sts of Back to Right Front.

With **right** side facing, place remaining {22-24}{26-28-30} Back sts onto st holder.

Instructions continued on page 6.

SLEEVE (Make 2)

SCALLOPED EDGING

Work First thru Third Scallops once, then repeat Second Scallop, {1-0}{0-0-0} time(s) **more**.

BODY

SIZE 2 ONLY

Joining Row: Add on 2 sts, P2, K2, P2, **turn**, add on 2 sts, **turn**, P2, K2, **turn**, add on 2 sts, **turn**, K2, P2, add on 2 sts, **turn**, P2, K2, **turn**, add on 2 sts: 26 sts.

SIZES 4, 6, 8, AND 10 ONLY

Joining Row: Add on 2 sts, K2, (P2, K2) across Scallop, **turn**, add on 2 sts, **turn**, (K2, P2) across Scallop, **turn**, add on 2 sts, **turn**, (P2, K2) across Scallop, **turn**, add on 2 sts: {32}{32-44-44} sts.

ALL SIZES

Row 1: K2, (P2, K2) across to last {0-2}{2-2-2} sts, P{0-2}{2-2-2}.

Row 2: K{0-2}{2-2-2}, P2, (K2, P2) across.

Work even for {0-2}{2-4-4} rows.

Next Row: Increase *(see Increases, page 30)*, work across to last st, increase: {28-34}{34-46-46} sts.

Maintaining pattern, continue to increase one stitch at **each** edge, every {2nd-4th}{4th-8th-6th} row, {4-5}{5-7-4} times **more**, then increase every {4th-6th}{6th-0-8th} row, {5-3}{5-0-5} times: {46-50}{54-60-64} sts.

Work even until Sleeve measures approximately {8-10}{12-13½-14¾}"/{20.5-25.5}{30.5-34.5-37.5} cm from cast on edge of Scallops, ending by working a **wrong** side row.

Bind off all sts in pattern.

FINISHING

Matching center of last row of Sleeve to shoulder joining, sew top of Sleeve to edge of Body, being careful not to catch armhole bound off sts.

Sew Sleeve edges to armhole bound off sts *(Fig. A)*.

Fig. A

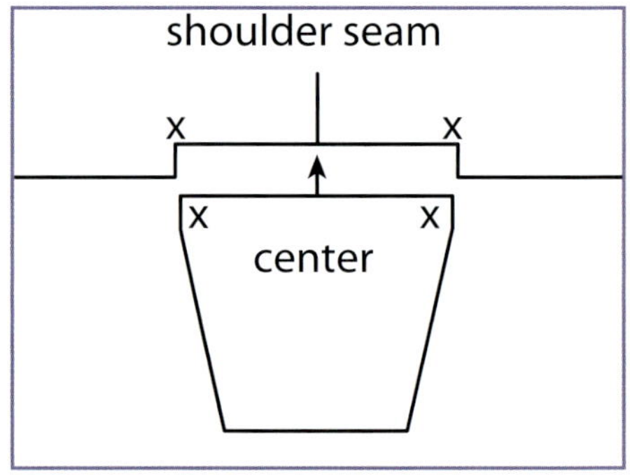

Weave Sleeve seam *(Fig. 12, page 31)*.

NECK BAND

Row 1: With **right** side facing and beginning at bound off edge on Neck Shaping, pick up {20-21}{22-23-24} sts along Right Front neck edge *(Fig. 11, page 31)*, K {22-24}{26-28-30} sts from Back neck st holder, pick up {20-21}{22-23-24} sts along Left Front neck edge: {62-66}{70-74-78} sts.

Row 2: P2, (K2, P2) across.

Row 3: K2, (P2, K2) across.

Row 4: P2, (K2, P2) across.

Bind off all sts **loosely** in pattern.

BUTTON BAND

Row 1: With **right** side facing and leaving end of rows on Scallop free, pick up {52-56}{60-64-68} sts along Left Front edge.

Rows 2-5: (K2, P2) across.

Bind off all sts **loosely** in pattern.

BUTTONHOLE BAND

Row 1: With **right** side facing and leaving end of rows on Scallop free, pick up {52-56}{60-64-68} sts along Right Front edge.

Rows 2 and 3: (K2, P2) across.

Mark placement of buttonholes on Buttonhole Band, always placing each marker before 2 knit sts and placing the first marker ½" (12 mm) from bottom of band and placing the last marker ½" (12 mm) from top of band; then evenly space {3-4}{4-5-5} more markers for remaining buttonholes.

Row 4 (Buttonhole row)**:** ★ Work across to next marker, YO *(Fig. 6b, page 30)*, K2 tog; repeat from ★ {4-5}{5-6-6} times **more**, work across.

Row 5: (K2, P2) across.

Bind off all sts **loosely** in pattern.

Sew buttons to Button Band opposite buttonholes.

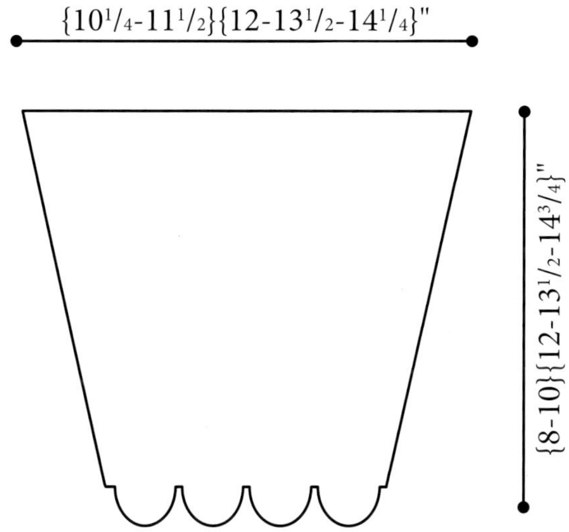

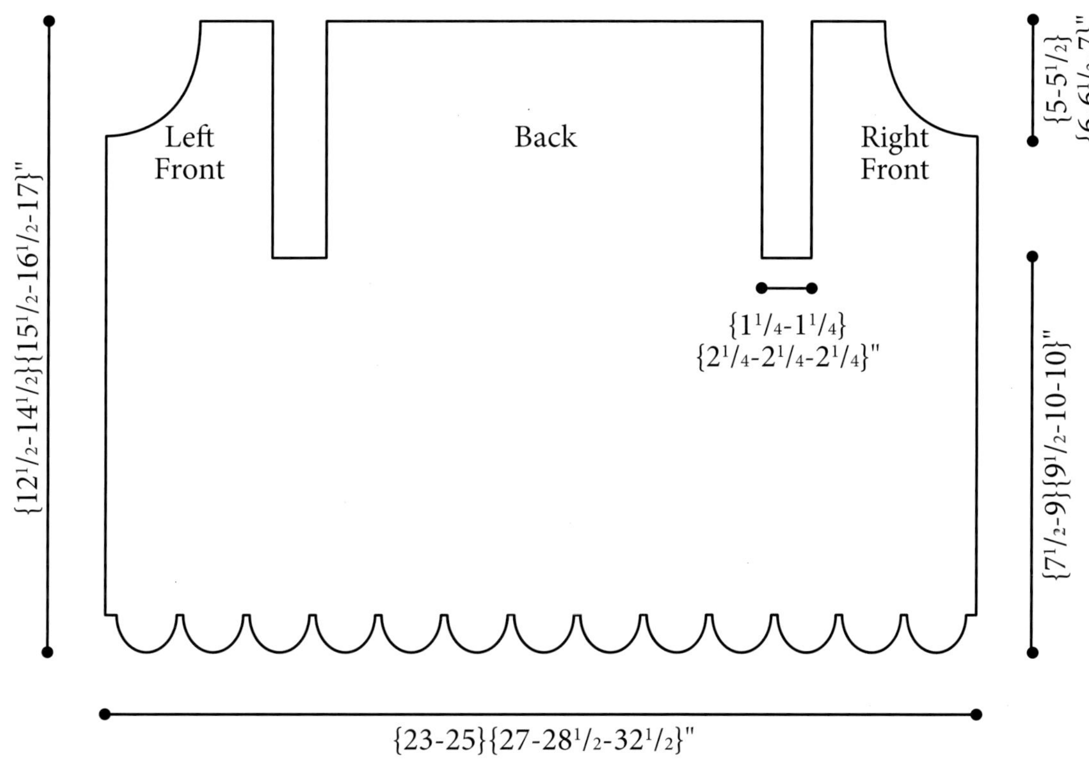

Note: Pieces include two edge stitches.

Striped Pullover

EASY

Size	Finished Chest Measurement	
2	25"	(63.5 cm)
4	26"	(66 cm)
6	27¹/₂"	(70 cm)
8	29¹/₄"	(74 cm)
10	31"	(78.5 cm)

Size Note: Instructions are written with sizes 2 and 4 in the first set of braces { } and sizes 6, 8, and 10 in the second set of braces. Instructions will be easier to read if you circle all the numbers pertaining to your size. If only one number is given, it applies to all sizes.

MATERIALS

MEDIUM 4

Medium Weight Yarn
[3¹/₂ ounces, 220 yards
(100 grams, 201 meters) per skein]:
Lt Pink - {1-2}{2-2-2} skein(s)
Medium Weight Mohair Yarn
[1³/₄ ounces, 126 yards
(50 grams, 115 meters) per skein]:
Pink - 2 skeins
Medium Weight Ribbon Yarn
[1³/₄ ounces, 110 yards
(50 grams, 101 meters) per skein]:
Variegated - {1-1}{2-2-3} skein(s)
Straight knitting needles, sizes 6 (4 mm) **and** 7 (4.5 mm) **or** sizes needed for gauge
16" (40.5 cm) Circular needle, size 7 (4.5 mm)
Double pointed needles, size 7 (4.5 mm)
Stitch holders - 2
Point protectors - 2
Yarn needle

GAUGE: With Lt Pink and larger size needles, in Stockinette Stitch,
18 sts and 24 rows = 4" (10 cm)

STITCH GUIDE

LOOP ST

K1, do **not** drop st from left needle. With right needle, pull loop just made to measure $^{1}/_{2}$" (12 mm) and drop off needle. Knit into **back** of same st on left needle *(Fig. A)*.

Fig. A

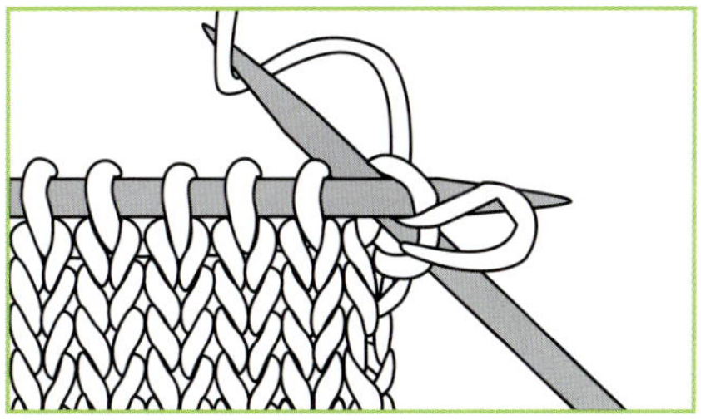

BACK

With Variegated and larger size needles, cast on {58-61}{64-68-72} sts.

Rows 1-4: Knit across.

Row 5 (Right side)**:** K1, work Loop St across to last st, K1, cut Variegated.

Rows 6-14: With Lt Pink and beginning with a **purl** row, work in Stockinette Stitch (purl one row, knit one row); at end of last row, cut Lt Pink.

Row 15: With Variegated, knit across; do **not** cut yarn.

Row 16: With Pink Mohair, purl across.

Row 17: Knit across; cut Pink Mohair.

Row 18: With Variegated, purl across; cut Variegated.

Rows 19-27: With Lt Pink and beginning with a **knit** row, work in Stockinette Stitch; at end of last row, cut Lt Pink.

Row 28: With Variegated, purl across; do **not** cut yarn.

Row 29: With Pink Mohair, knit across.

Row 30: Purl across; cut Pink Mohair.

Row 31: With Variegated, knit across; cut Variegated.

Repeat Rows 6-31 for pattern until Back measures approximately {7$^{1}/_{2}$-8}{8$^{1}/_{2}$-9-9$^{1}/_{2}$}"/{19-20.5}{21.5-23-24} cm from cast on edge, ending by working a **purl** row.

ARMHOLE SHAPING

Maintain established pattern throughout.

Rows 1 and 2: Bind off {2-3}{4-5-4} sts, work across: {54-55}{56-58-64} sts.

Work even until Armholes measure approximately {5$^{1}/_{2}$-6}{6$^{1}/_{2}$-7-7$^{1}/_{2}$}"/{14-15}{16.5-18-19} cm, ending by working a **knit** row.

NECK SHAPING

Row 1: P {36-40}{40-42-45}, slip {18-25}{24-26-26} sts just worked onto st holder, purl across: {18-15}{16-16-19} sts **each** side.

Both sides of neck are worked at same time, using a separate ball of yarn for each side.

Row 2: Knit across to within 2 sts of neck edge, SSK *(Figs. 8a-c, page 31)*, cut yarn and slip sts just made onto circular needle; with second yarn, K2 tog *(Fig. 7, page 30)*, knit across, cut yarn and slip sts just made onto circular needle, place point protectors on ends: {17-14}{15-15-18} sts **each** side.

FRONT

Work same as Back until Armholes measure approximately {3-3$^{1}/_{2}$}{4-4-4$^{1}/_{2}$}"/{7.5-9}{10-10-11.5} cm, ending by working a **purl** row.

Instructions continued on page 10.

NECK SHAPING

Both sides of neck are worked at same time, using a separate ball of yarn for each side.

Row 1: K {24-23}{24-24-27}, slip next {6-9}{8-10-10} sts onto st holder; with second yarn, knit across: {24-23}{24-24-27} sts **each** side.

Rows 2 and 3: Work across; with second yarn, bind off 2 sts, work across: {22-21}{22-22-25} sts **each** side.

Repeat Rows 2 and 3, {0-1}{1-1-1} time(s) *(see Zeros, page 30)*: {22-19}{20-20-23} sts **each** side.

Next Row: Purl across; with second yarn, purl across.

Next Row (Decrease row)**:** Knit across to within 2 sts of neck edge, SSK; with second yarn, K2 tog, knit across: {21-18}{19-19-22} sts each side.

Repeat last two rows, 4 times: {17-14}{15-15-18} sts **each** side.

Work even until Front measures same as Back, ending by working a **knit** row.

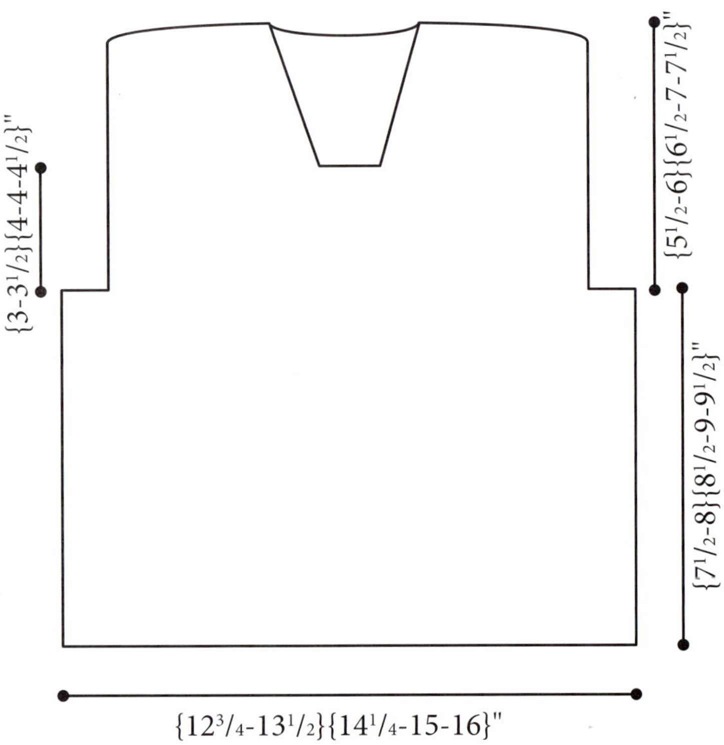

SHOULDER JOINING

Using 3-Needle Bind Off *(Fig. 10, page 31)*, join Right Front shoulder sts to Back; with second yarn, join Left Front shoulder sts to Back.

SLEEVE (Make 2)

With Variegated and smaller size needles, cast on {27-29}{31-31-33} sts.

Rows 1-4: Knit across.

Row 5 (Right side)**:** K1, work Loop St in each st across to last st, K1, cut Variegated.

Row 6: With Pink Mohair, knit across.

Row 7: Purl across.

Row 8: Knit increase *(Figs. 3a & b, page 30)*, knit across to last st, knit increase: {29-31}{33-33-35} sts.

Working in Reverse Stockinette Stitch, continue to increase one stitch at **each** edge, every {2nd-2nd}{4th-4th-4th} row, {5-1}{13-15-17} time(s) **more**; then increase every {4-4}{0-0-0} rows, {6-11}{0-0-0} times: {51-55}{59-63-69} sts.

Work even until Sleeve measures approximately {8-10}{11-12 1/2-13 1/2}"/{20.5-25.5}{28-32-34.5} cm from cast on edge.

Bind off all sts.

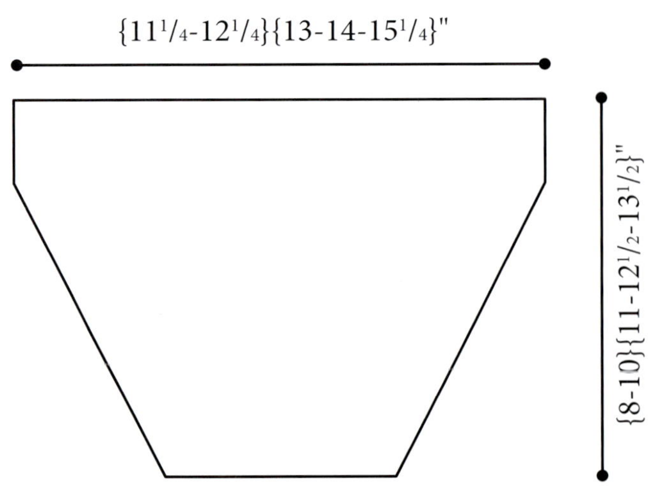

Note: Pieces include two edge stitches.

FINISHING

Matching center of last row on Sleeve to shoulder joining and beginning {5¼-5¾}{6¼-6½-7}"/ {13.5-14.5}{16-16.5-18} cm down from joining, sew top of Sleeve to Sweater.

Sew Sleeve edges to armhole bound off sts *(Fig. A, page 6)*.

With Lt Pink, weave underarm and side in one continuous seam *(Fig. 12, page 31)*.

NECK EDGING

With **right** side facing, using Light Pink, and circular needle, pick up {15-15}{17-19-19} sts evenly spaced across left Neck edge *(Fig. 11, page 31)*, slip {6-9}{8-10-10} sts from Front st holder onto second end of needle and knit across, pick up {15-15}{17-19-19} sts evenly spaced across right Neck edge, knit {18-25}{24-26-26} sts from Back st holder, place marker to mark beginning of rnd *(see Markers, page 28)*; cut Lt Pink: {54-64}{66-74-74} sts.

Rnd 1: With Variegated, (K1, P1) around.

Rnd 2: (P1, K1) around.

Bind off all sts **loosely** in pattern.

Twisted Trim Cardigan

EASY

Size	Finished Chest Measurement	
2	24½"	(62 cm)
4	29"	(73.5 cm)
6	30"	(76 cm)
8	34½"	(87.5 cm)
10	36"	(91.5 cm)

Size Note: Instructions are written with sizes 2 and 4 in the first set of braces { } and sizes 6, 8, and 10 in the second set of braces. Instructions will be easier to read if you circle all the numbers pertaining to your size. If only one number is given, it applies to all sizes.

MATERIALS

Medium Weight Yarn (MEDIUM 4)
[3½ ounces, 191 yards
(100 grams, 175 meters) per skein]:
Pink - {2-3}{3-4-4} skeins
Medium Weight Yarn
[1¾ ounces, 85 yards
(50 grams, 78 meters) per hank]:
Variegated - {5-6}{7-8-9} hanks
Straight knitting needles, size 10½ (6.5 mm)
or size needed for gauge
32" (81.5 cm) Circular needle, size 10½ (6.5 mm)
Stitch holder
Large snap
Large button or flower - optional
Point protectors - 2

Cardigan is worked holding one strand of Pink and one strand of Variegated together throughout.

GAUGE: In Stockinette Stitch,
14 sts and 20 rows = 4" (10 cm)

BACK

With circular needle, cast on {46-51}{56-61-66} sts.

Row 1: Knit across.

Row 2: Purl across.

Rows 3 and 4: Repeat Rows 1 and 2.

Row 5: ★ K5, rotate left needle counterclockwise 360 degrees *(Fig. A)*; repeat from ★ across to last st, K1.

Fig. A

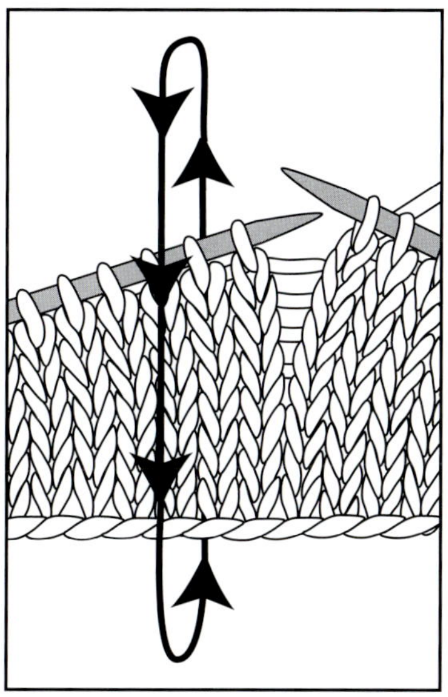

Row 6: Purl across.

Row 7 (Right side)**:** Knit across.

Beginning with a **purl** row, work even in Stockinette Stitch until Back measures approximately {$12^{1}/_{2}$-$13^{1}/_{2}$}{$14^{1}/_{2}$-$16^{1}/_{2}$-$17^{1}/_{2}$}"/{32-34.5}{37-42-44.5} cm from bottom edge, ending by working a **knit** row.

Leave stitches on circular needle; cut yarn leaving a long end for 3-Needle Bind Off. Place point protectors on circular needle.

RIGHT FRONT

With straight needles, cast on {21-26}{26-31-31} sts.

Row 1: Knit across.

Row 2: Purl across.

Rows 3 and 4: Repeat Rows 1 and 2.

Row 5: ★ K5, rotate left needle counterclockwise 360 degrees; repeat from ★ across to last st, K1.

Row 6: Purl across.

Row 7 (Right side)**:** Knit across.

Beginning with a **purl** row, work even in Stockinette Stitch until Right Front measures approximately {$9^{1}/_{2}$-$10^{1}/_{2}$}{$11^{1}/_{2}$-$13^{1}/_{2}$-$14^{1}/_{2}$}"/{24-26.5}{29-34.5-37} cm from bottom edge, ending by working a **purl** row.

NECK SHAPING

Row 1: Bind off {6-5}{6-5-6} sts, knit across: {15-21}{20-26-25} sts.

Row 2: Purl across.

Row 3 (Decrease row)**:** SSK *(Figs. 8a-c, page 31)*, knit across: {14-20}{19-25-24} sts.

Repeat Rows 2 and 3, {2-4}{2-5-3} times: {12-16}{17-20-21} sts.

Work even until Right Front measures same as Back, ending by working a **knit** row.

SHOULDER JOINING

Using 3-Needle Bind Off *(Fig. 10, page 31)*, join Right Front to first {12-16}{17-20-21} sts of Back. Leave remaining {22-19}{22-21-24} Back sts on circular needle and replace point protector.

Instructions continued on page 14.

LEFT FRONT

Work same as Right Front to Neck Shaping, ending by working a **knit** row.

NECK SHAPING

Row 1: Bind off {6-5}{6-5-6} sts, purl across: {15-21}{20-26-25} sts.

Row 2 (Decrease row)**:** Knit across to last 2 sts, K2 tog: {14-20}{19-25-24} sts.

Row 3: Purl across.

Repeat Rows 2 and 3, {2-4}{2-5-3} times: {12-16}{17-20-21} sts.

Work even until Left Front measures same as Back, ending by working a **purl** row.

SHOULDER JOINING

Using long end from Back and 3-Needle Bind Off, join Left Front to last {12-16}{17-20-21} sts of Back. Slip remaining Back sts onto st holder.

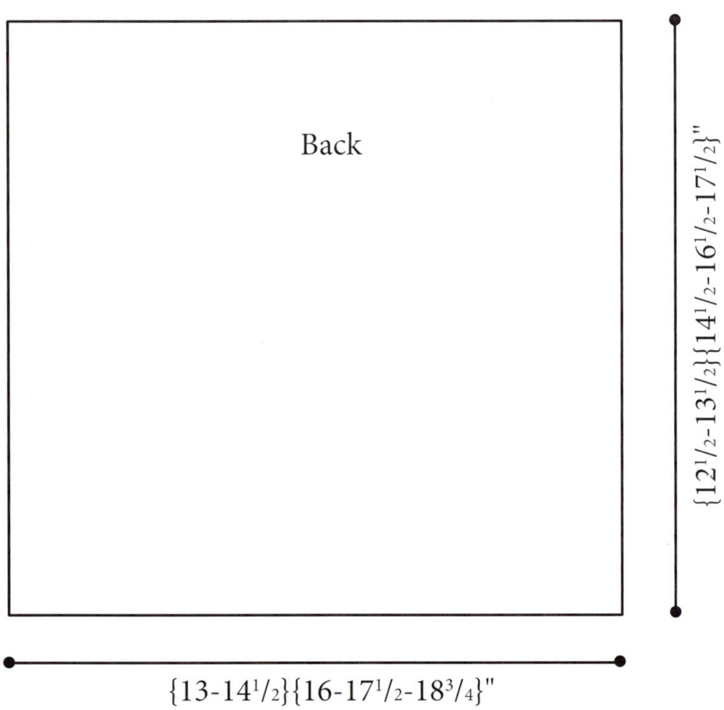

SLEEVE (Make 2)

With straight needles, cast on {26-26}{31-31-36} sts.

Row 1: Knit across.

Row 2: Purl across.

Rows 3 and 4: Repeat Rows 1 and 2.

Row 5: ★ K5, rotate left needle counterclockwise 360 degrees; repeat from ★ across to last st, K1.

Row 6: Purl across.

Row 7 (Right side)**:** Knit across.

Row 8: Purl across.

Row 9: Increase *(see Increases, page 30)*, knit across to last st, increase: {28-28}{33-33-38} sts.

Working in Stockinette Stitch, continue to increase one stitch at each edge in same manner, every {4th-4th}{6th-4th-6th} row, {3-7}{6-6-4} times **more**; then increase every {6th-6th}{0-6th-8th} row *(see Zeros, page 30)*, {2-1}{0-3-3} time(s): {38-44}{45-51-52} sts.

Work even until Sleeve measures approximately {8$^{1}/_{2}$-10$^{1}/_{2}$}{11$^{1}/_{2}$-12$^{1}/_{2}$-14}"/{21.5-26.5}{29-32-35.5} cm from bottom edge, ending by working a **purl** row.

Bind off all sts in **knit**.

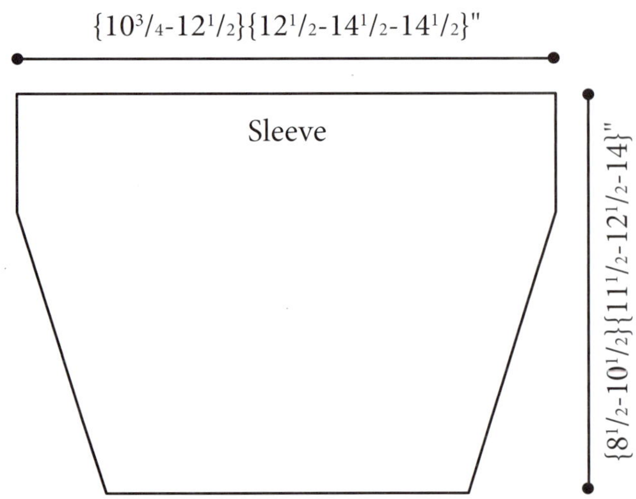

Note: Pieces include two edge stitches.

FINISHING
RUFFLED EDGING

With **right** side facing and circular needle, pick up {34-39}{43-48-55} sts along Right Front edge *(Fig. 11, page 31)*, pick up {17-17}{17-17-18} sts along Right neck edge, knit {22-19}{22-21-24} sts from Back neck stitch holder, pick up {18-17}{18-18-18} sts along Left neck edge, pick up {34-39}{43-48-55} sts along Left Front edge: {125-131}{143-152-170} sts.

Row 1: Purl across.

Row 2: Bind off 2 sts, ★ slip st from right needle onto left needle, add on 2 sts *(Figs. 5a & b, page 30)*, bind off 4 sts; repeat from ★ across.

Sew Sleeves to Sweater, matching center of last row on Sleeve to shoulder joining and beginning {5½-6¼}{6½-7¼-7½}"/{14-16}{16.5-18.5-19} cm down from joining.

Weave underarm and side in one continuous seam *(Fig. 12, page 31)*.

Sew snap to corner of neck edge. Add flower or button to Left Front to cover Snap.

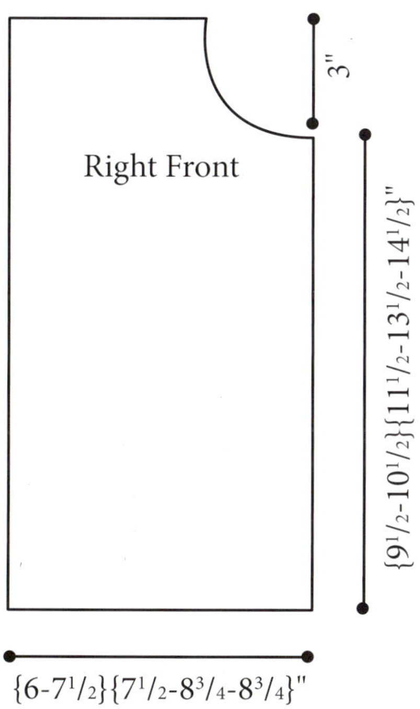

Eyelet Cardigan

INTERMEDIATE

Size	Finished Chest Measurement	
2	24 1/4"	(61.5 cm)
4	27 1/2"	(70 cm)
6	30 1/2"	(77.5 cm)
8	34"	(86.5 cm)
10	37 1/4"	(94.5 cm)

Size Note: Instructions are written with sizes 2 and 4 in the first set of braces { } and sizes 6, 8, and 10 in the second set of braces. Instructions will be easier to read if you circle all the numbers pertaining to your size. If only one number is given, it applies to all sizes.

MATERIALS

Medium Weight Yarn (MEDIUM 4)
  [3 1/2 ounces, 191 yards
    (100 grams, 175 meters) per skein]:
      Green - {2-3}{3-4-4} skeins
      Blue - 1 skein

Straight knitting needles, size 7 (4.5 mm) **or** size needed for gauge

Double pointed needles, size 7 (4.5 mm)

Yarn needle

GAUGE: In Stockinette Stitch,
20 sts and 24 rows = 4" (10 cm)

BACK

With Green and straight needles, cast on {63-71} {79-87-95} sts.

Row 1: Purl across.

Row 2: Knit across.

Row 3: Purl across.

Row 4 (Right side)**:** K3, YO *(Fig. 6a, page 30)*, K2 tog *(Fig. 7, page 30)*, (K6, YO, K2 tog) across to last 2 sts, K2.

Row 5: Purl across.

Row 6: K1, K2 tog, YO, K1, YO, K2 tog, ★ K3, K2 tog, YO, K1, YO, K2 tog; repeat from ★ across to last st, K1.

Row 7: Purl across.

Row 8: Knit across.

Rows 9-11: Repeat Rows 7 and 8 once, then repeat Row 7 once **more**.

Row 12: K7, (YO, K2 tog, K6) across.

Row 13: Purl across.

Row 14: K5, K2 tog, YO, K1, YO, K2 tog, ★ K3, K2 tog, YO, K1, YO, K2 tog; repeat from ★ across to last 5 sts, K5.

Row 15: Purl across.

Row 16: Knit across.

Rows 17-19: Repeat Rows 15 and 16 once, then repeat Row 15 once **more**.

Repeat Rows 4-19 until Back measures approximately {8-9}{10-11-11½}"/{20.5-23}{25.5-28-29} cm from cast on edge, ending by working a **right** side row.

ARMHOLE SHAPING

Maintain established pattern throughout.

Rows 1 and 2: Bind off {5-5}{5-6-7} sts, work across: {53-61}{69-75-81} sts.

Row 3: Purl across.

Row 4 (Decrease row)**:** SSK *(Figs. 8a-c, page 31)*, work across to last 2 sts, K2 tog: {51-59}{67-73-79} sts.

Repeat Rows 3 and 4, {3-3}{3-4-6} times: {45-53} {61-65-67} sts.

Work even until Back measures approximately {13-14½}{16-17-18½}"/{33-37}{40.5-43-47} cm from cast on edge, ending by working a **purl** row.

SHOULDER SHAPING

Rows 1 and 2: Bind off {3-3}{3-4-4} sts, work across: {39-47}{55-57-59} sts.

Rows 3 and 4: Bind off {3-3}{4-4-5} sts, work across: {33-41}{47-49-49} sts.

Rows 5 and 6: Bind off {3-4}{4-5-5} sts, work across: {27-33}{39-39-39} sts.

Bind off remaining sts in **knit**.

RIGHT FRONT

With Green and straight needles, cast on {31-35} {39-43-47} sts.

Row 1: Purl across.

Row 2: Knit across.

Row 3: Purl across.

Row 4 (Right side)**:** K3, YO, K2 tog, (K6, YO, K2 tog) across to last {2-6}{2-6-2} sts, knit across.

Instructions continued on page 18.

Row 5: Purl across.

Row 6: K1, K2 tog, YO, K1, YO, K2 tog, ★ K3, K2 tog, YO, K1, YO, K2 tog; repeat from ★ across to last {1-5} {1-5-1} st(s), knit across.

Row 7: Purl across.

Row 8: Knit across.

Rows 9-11: Repeat Rows 7 and 8 once, then repeat Row 7 once **more**.

Row 12: K7, YO, K2 tog, (K6, YO, K2 tog) across to last {6-2}{6-2-6} sts, knit across.

Row 13: Purl across.

Row 14: K5, K2 tog, YO, K1, YO, K2 tog, ★ K3, K2 tog, YO, K1, YO, K2 tog; repeat from ★ across to last {5-1} {5-1-5} st(s), knit across.

Row 15: Purl across.

Row 16: Knit across.

Rows 17-19: Repeat Rows 15 and 16 once, then repeat Row 15 once **more**.

Repeat Rows 4-19 until Right Front measures same as Back to Armhole Shaping, ending by working a **right** side row.

ARMHOLE SHAPING

Maintain established pattern throughout.

Row 1: Bind off {5-5}{5-6-7} sts, purl across: {26-30} {34-37-40} sts.

Row 2: Work across.

Row 3: Purl across.

Row 4 (Decrease row)**:** Work across to last 2 sts, K2 tog: {25-29}{33-36-39} sts.

Repeat Rows 3 and 4, {3-3}{3-4-6} times: {22-26} {30-32-33} sts.

Work even until Right Front measures approximately {11-12}{13-14-15½}"/{28-30.5}{33-35.5-39.5} cm from cast on edge, ending by working a **purl** row.

NECK SHAPING

Row 1: Bind off {4-7}{10-10-10} sts, work across: {18-19}{20-22-23} sts.

Row 2: Purl across.

Row 3 (Decrease row): Bind off 2 sts, work across: {16-17}{18-20-21} sts.

Rows 4 and 5: Repeat Rows 2 and 3: {14-15} {16-18-19} sts.

Row 6: Purl across.

Row 7 (Decrease row): SSK, work across: {13-14} {15-17-18} sts.

Rows 8-15: Repeat Rows 6 and 7, 4 times: {9-10} {11-13-14} sts.

Work even until Armhole measures {5-5½}{6-6-7}"/ {12.5-14}{15-15-18} cm, ending by working a **right** side row.

SHOULDER SHAPING

Row 1: Bind off {3-3}{3-4-4} sts, purl across: {6-7} {8-9-10} sts.

Row 2: Work across.

Row 3: Bind off {3-3}{4-4-5} sts, purl across: {3-4} {4-5-5} sts.

Row 4: Work across.

Bind off remaining sts in **purl**.

Instructions continued on page 20.

FROM THE DIRECTOR OF
SweeTARTS

LEFT FRONT

With Green and straight needles, cast on {31-35} {39-43-47} sts.

Row 1: Purl across.

Row 2: Knit across.

Row 3: Purl across.

Row 4: K{2-6}{2-6-2}, YO, K2 tog, (K6, YO, K2 tog) across to last 3 sts, K3.

Row 5: Purl across.

Row 6: K{0-4}{0-4-0} *(see Zeros, page 29)*, K2 tog, YO, K1, YO, K2 tog, ★ K3, K2 tog, YO, K1, YO, K2 tog; repeat from ★ across to last 2 sts, K2.

Row 7: Purl across.

Row 8: Knit across.

Rows 9-11: Repeat Rows 7 and 8 once, then repeat Row 7 once **more**.

Row 12: K{6-2}{6-2-6}, YO, K2 tog, (K6, YO, K2 tog) across to last 7 sts, K7.

Row 13: Purl across.

Row 14: K{4-0}{4-0-4}, K2 tog, YO, K1, YO, K2 tog, ★ K3, K2 tog, YO, K1, YO, K2 tog; repeat from ★ across to last 6 sts, K6.

Row 15: Purl across.

Row 16: Knit across.

Rows 17-19: Repeat Rows 15 and 16 once, then repeat Row 15 once **more**.

Repeat Rows 4-19 until Left Front measures same as Right Front to Armhole Shaping, ending by working a **purl** row.

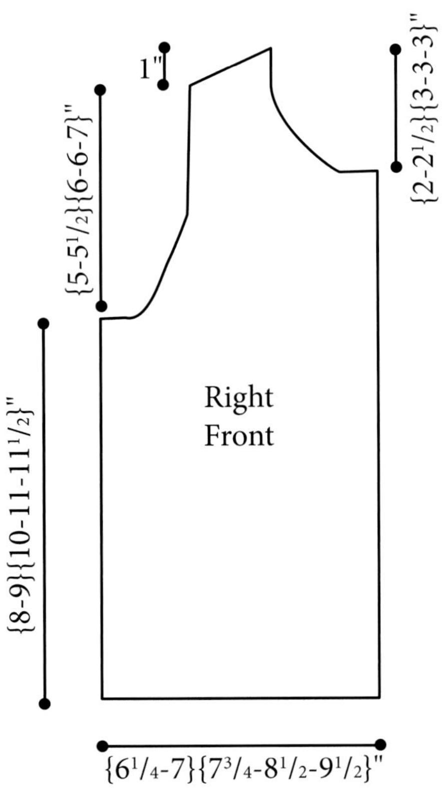

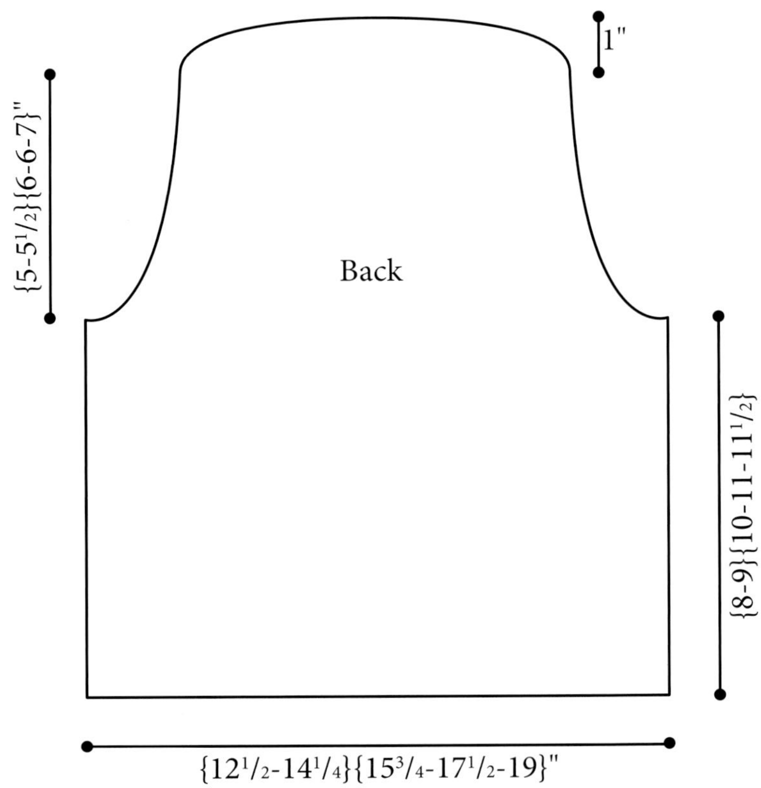

Note: Pieces include two edge stitches.

ARMHOLE SHAPING

Maintain established pattern throughout.

Row 1: Bind off {5-5}{5-6-7} sts, work across: {26-30}{34-37-40} sts.

Row 2: Purl across.

Row 3 (Decrease row)**:** SSK, work across: {25-29}{33-36-39} sts.

Rows 4 thru {9-9}{9-11-15}: Repeat Rows 2 and 3, {3-3}{3-4-6} times: {22-26}{30-32-33} sts.

Work even until Left Front measures same as Right Front to Neck Shaping, ending by working a **right** side row.

NECK SHAPING

Row 1: Bind off {4-7}{10-10-10} sts, purl across: {18-19}{20-22-23} sts.

Row 2: Work across.

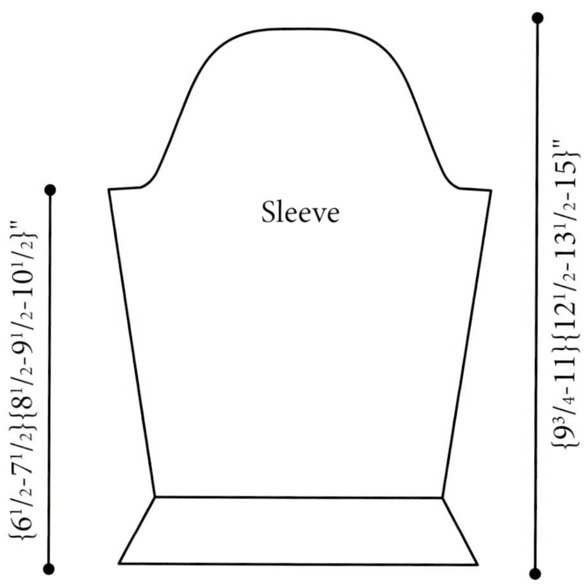

Row 3 (Decrease row)**:** Bind off 2 sts, purl across: {16-17}{18-20-21} sts.

Rows 4 and 5: Repeat Rows 2 and 3: {14-15}{16-18-19} sts.

Row 6 (Decrease row)**:** Work across to last 2 sts, K2 tog: {13-14}{15-17-18} sts.

Row 7: Purl across.

Rows 8-14: Repeat Rows 6 and 7, 3 times; then repeat Row 6 once **more:** {9-10}{11-13-14} sts.

Work even until Left Front measures same as Right Front to Shoulder Shaping, ending by working a **purl** row.

SHOULDER SHAPING

Row 1: Bind off {3-3}{3-4-4} sts, work across: {6-7}{8-9-10} sts.

Row 2: Purl across.

Row 3: Bind off {3-3}{4-4-5} sts, work across: {3-4}{4-5-5} sts.

Row 4: Purl across.

Bind off remaining sts in **knit.**

SLEEVE (Make 2)

Cast on {62-78}{78-94-94} sts.

Row 1 (Right side)**:** Knit across.

Row 2: Purl across.

Rows 3-8: Repeat Rows 1 and 2, 3 times.

Row 9: K2 tog across: {31-39}{39-47-47} sts.

Instructions continued on page 22.

Row 10: Purl across.

Row 11: K3, YO, K2 tog, (K6, YO, K2 tog) across to last 2 sts, K2.

Row 12: Purl across.

Row 13: K1, K2 tog, YO, K1, YO, K2 tog, ★ K3, K2 tog, YO, K1, YO, K2 tog; repeat from ★ across to last st, K1.

Row 14: Purl across.

Row 15: Knit increase *(Figs. 3a & b, page 30)*, knit across to last st, knit increase: {33-41}{41-49-49} sts.

Row 16: Purl across.

Row 17: Knit across.

Row 18: Purl across.

Row 19: K8, YO, K2 tog, (K6, YO, K2 tog) across to last 7 sts, K7.

Row 20: Purl across.

Row 21 (Increase row): Knit increase, K5, K2 tog, YO, K1, YO, K2 tog, ★ K3, K2 tog, YO, K1, YO, K2 tog; repeat from ★ across to last 6 sts, K5, knit increase: {35-43}{43-51-51} sts.

Maintaining established pattern, continue to increase one stitch at each edge, every 6 rows, {3-4}{5-6-7} times **more**: {41-51}{53-63-65} sts.

Work even until Sleeve measures approximately {6½-7½}{8½-9½-10½}"/{16.5-19}{21.5-24-26.5} cm from cast on edge, ending by working a **right** side row.

SLEEVE CAP

Rows 1 and 2: Bind off {5-5}{5-6-7} sts, work across: {31-41}{43-51-51} sts.

Row 3: Purl across.

Row 4 (Decrease row): SSK, work across to last 2 sts, K2 tog: {29-39}{41-49-49} sts.

Rows 5 thru {10-10}{10-12-16}: Repeat Rows 3 and 4, {3-3}{3-4-6} times: {23-33}{35-41-37} sts.

Row {11-11}{11-13-17}: P2 tog *(Fig. 9, page 31)*, purl across: {22-32}{34-40-36} sts.

Row {12-12}{12-14-18}: SSK, work across: {21-31}{33-39-35} sts.

Repeat last 2 rows, {4-5}{6-5-5} times: {13-21}{21-29-25} sts.

Next 2 Rows: Bind off {2-3}{3-4-3} sts, work across: {9-15}{15-21-19} sts.

Bind off remaining sts.

FINISHING

Sew shoulder seams.

Sew Sleeves to Cardigan, placing center stitch of Sleeve Cap at shoulder seam.

Weave underarm and side in one continuous seam *(Fig. 12, page 31)*.

I-CORD TRIM

With Blue and double pointed needles, cast on 4 sts, ★ K4, do **not** turn, slide the stitches to the opposite end of the needle; repeat from ★ until cord measures desired finished length.

Sleeves: Make I-cord to fit around cuff of Sleeves. Sew in place stretching I-cord slightly.

Body: Make I-cord to fit around Front and bottom edges. Sew in place stretching I-cord slightly.

Neck: Make I-cord 22" (56 cm) longer than Neck edge. Beginning 11" (28 cm) from one end (tie), sew to Neck edge stretching slightly and leaving 11" (28 cm) free at opposite end (tie).

Note: Since I-cords can be hard to measure, knit them longer than needed. Place the stitches on a stitch holder and begin sewing in place. Place the stitches back on the needles to shorten or lenghten to fit and to bind off.

Ruffled Pullover

INTERMEDIATE

Size	Finished Chest Measurement	
2	22"	(56 cm)
4	26½"	(67.5 cm)
6	31"	(78.5 cm)
8	35½"	(90 cm)
10	40"	(101.5 cm)

Size Note: Instructions are written with sizes 2 and 4 in the first set of braces { } and sizes 6, 8, and 10 in the second set of braces. Instructions will be easier to read if you circle all the numbers pertaining to your size. If only one number is given, it applies to all sizes.

MATERIALS

Medium Weight Yarn
[3½ ounces, 220 yards
(100 grams, 201 meters) per skein]:
Fuchsia - {2-2}{3-3-3} skeins
[1¾ ounces, 100 yards
(50 grams, 91 meters) per skein]:
Light Blue - 1 skein
Medium Weight Mohair Yarn
[.88 ounce, 108 yards
(25 grams, 100 meters) per skein]:
Pink - 1 skein
Medium Weight Novelty Eyelash Yarn
[1¾ ounces, 28 yards
(50 grams, 26 meters) per skein]:
Variegated - 2 skeins
Straight knitting needles, size 7 (4.5 mm) **or** size needed for gauge
16" (40.5 cm) Circular needle, size 5 (3.75 mm)
Bobbins
Stitch holder
Yarn needle
Point protectors - 2

GAUGE: In Stockinette Stitch,
18 sts and 25 rows = 4" (10 cm)

Instructions begin on page 24.

BACK

With circular needles and Fuchsia, cast on {205-245}{285-325-365} sts.

Row 1 (Right side)**:** K3, with left needle pass second st on right needle over first st and off the needle, ★ K2, with left needle pass second st on right needle over first st and off the needle; repeat from ★ across: {103-123}{143-163-183} sts.

Row 2: P1, [P2 tog *(Fig. 9, page 31)*] across: {52-62}{72-82-92} sts.

Change to larger size needles.

Rows 3-10: Beginning with a **knit** row, work 8 rows in Stockinette Stitch (knit one row, purl one row); at end of last row, cut Fuchsia.

Row 11: With Variegated, knit across; cut Variegated.

Row 12: With Fuchsia, purl across.

Row 13: Knit across.

Row 14: Purl across.

Row 15: K1, follow Chart A, page 27 across to last st, K1.

Row 16: P1, follow Chart A across to last st, P1.

Rows 17-22: Repeat Rows 15 and 16, 3 times.

Rows 23-26: With Fuchsia, repeat Rows 13 and 14 twice; at end of Row 26, cut Fuchsia.

Row 27: With Variegated, knit across; cut Variegated.

Row 28: With Fuchsia, purl across.

Work even in Stockinette Stitch until Back measures approximately {12-12½}{13½-15½-16½}"/{30.5-32}{34.5-39.5-42} cm from bottom edge, ending by working a **knit** row; cut yarn leaving a long end for 3-Needle Bind Off.

Slip sts onto circular needle.

FRONT

Work same as Back until Front measures approximately {9-9½}{10½-12½-13½}"/{23-24}{26.5-32-34.5} cm from cast on edge, ending by working a **purl** row.

NECK SHAPING

Row 1: K {31-38}{43-48-53}, slip {10-14}{14-14-14} sts just worked onto st holder, knit across: {21-24}{29-34-39} sts **each** side.

Both sides of Neck are worked at same time, using a separate ball of yarn for each side.

Row 2: Purl across; with second yarn, purl across.

Row 3 (Decrease row)**:** Knit across to within 2 sts of Neck edge, K2 tog *(Fig. 7, page 30)*; with second yarn, SSK *(Figs. 8a-c, page 31)*, knit across: {20-23}{28-33-38} sts **each** side.

Repeat Rows 2 and 3, {4-5}{5-6-6} times: {16-18}{23-27-32} sts **each** side.

Work even until Front measures same as Back, ending by working a **knit** row.

RIGHT SHOULDER JOINING

Using 3-Needle Bind Off *(Fig. 10, page 31)*, join Right Front shoulder sts to first {16-18}{23-27-32} sts on Back.

LEFT SHOULDER JOINING

Using long end from Back and 3-Needle Bind Off, join Back to Left Front shoulder sts; leave remaining {20-26}{26-28-28} Back sts on circular needle.

SLEEVE (Make 2)

With Fuchsia, cast on {125-125}{165-165-165} sts.

Row 1 (Right side)**:** K3, with left needle pass second st on right needle over first st and off the needle, ★ K2, with left needle pass second st on right needle over first st and off the needle; repeat from ★ across: {63-63}{83-83-83} sts.

Row 2: P1, P2 tog across: {32-32}{42-42-42} sts.

Change to larger size needles.

Row 3: Knit across.

Row 4: Purl across.

Row 5: Knit increase *(Figs. 3a &b, page 30)*, knit across to last st, knit increase: {34-34}{44-44-44} sts.

Rows 6-8: Beginning with a **purl** row, work 3 rows in Stockinette Stitch.

Row 9: Knit increase, knit across to last st, knit increase: {36-36}{46-46-46} sts.

Row 10: Purl across; cut Fuchsia.

Row 11: With Variegated, knit across; cut Variegated.

Row 12: With Fuchsia, purl across.

Row 13: Knit increase, knit across to last st, knit increase: {38-38}{48-48-48} sts.

Row 14: Purl across.

Row 15: K4, follow Chart B, page 27 across to last 4 sts, K4.

Row 16: P4, follow Chart B across to last 4 sts, P4.

Row 17: Knit increase, K3, follow Chart B across to last 4 sts, K3, knit increase: {40-40}{50-50-50} sts.

Row 18: P5, follow Chart B across to last 5 sts, P5.

Row 19: K5, follow Chart B across to last 5 sts, K5.

Row 20: P5, follow Chart B across to last 5 sts, P5.

Row 21: Knit increase, K4, follow Chart B across to last 5 sts, K4, knit increase: {42-42}{52-52-52} sts.

Row 22: P6, follow Chart B across to last 6 sts, P6.

Row 23: With Fuchsia, knit across.

Row 24: Purl across.

Row 25: Knit increase, knit across to last st, knit increase: {44-44}{54-54-54} sts.

Row 26: Purl across; cut Fuchsia.

Row 27: With Variegated, knit across; cut Variegated.

Row 28: With Fuchsia, purl across.

Row 29: Knit increase, knit across to last st, knit increase: {46-46}{56-56-56} sts.

Continue to increase one stitch at **each** edge in same manner, every {4th-6th}{6th-6th-6th} row, {2-4}{1-1-4} time(s): {50-54}{58-58-64} sts.
Work even until Sleeve measures approximately {8-10}{11-12$^{1}/_{2}$-13$^{1}/_{2}$}"/{20.5-25.5}{28-32-34.5} cm from cast on edge.

Bind off all sts.

FINISHING

Sew Sleeves to Sweater, matching center of last row on Sleeve to shoulder joining and beginning {5$^{1}/_{2}$-6}{6$^{1}/_{2}$-6$^{1}/_{2}$-7}"/{12.5-15}{16.5-16.5-18} cm down from joining.

Weave underarm and side in one continuous seam *(Fig. 12, page 31)*.

NECK RIBBING

With **right** side facing, using Fuchsia and circular needle, pick up {15-16}{16-15-17} sts along left Front neck edge *(Fig. 11, page 31)*, knit {10-14}{14-14-14} from Front st holder, pick up {15-16}{16-15-17} sts along right Front neck edge, knit across Back neck sts, place marker to mark beginning of rnd *(see Markers, page 28)*: {60-72}{72-72-76} sts.

Rnd 1: Knit around.

Rnds 2-5: (With Blue, K2, with Fuchsia, P2) around.

Cut Blue.

Rnd 6: With Fuchsia, knit around, increasing {2-2}{2-2-1} st(s) evenly spaced: {62-74}{74-74-77} sts.

Rnd 7: Bind off 2 sts, ★ slip st from right needle onto left needle, add on 2 sts *(Figs. 5a & b, page 30)*, bind off 4 sts; repeat from ★ around

FOLLOWING A CHART

Following a chart can be easier than following written instructions. With a chart, you can see what the pattern looks like. The chart shows each stitch as a square indicating what color each stitch should be. Visualize the chart as your fabric, beginning at the bottom edge.

For ease in following the chart, place a ruler on the chart under the row being worked to help keep your place *(see Changing Colors and Bobbin Knitting, page 29)*.

Key

☐ Fuchsia

☐ (|) Light Blue

☐ (×) Pink Mohair

CHART A

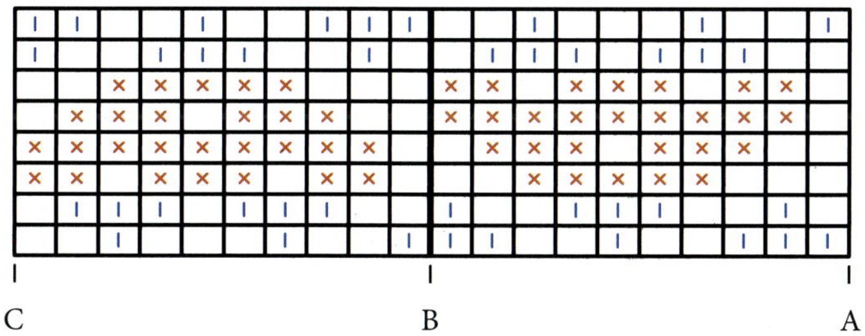

Chart A

On **right** side rows, work from A to C {2-3}{3-4-4} times, then from A to B {1-0}{1-0-1} time(s) *(see Zeros, page 29)*.

On **wrong** side rows, work from B to A {1-0}{1-0-1} time(s), then from C to A {2-3}{3-4-4} times.

CHART B

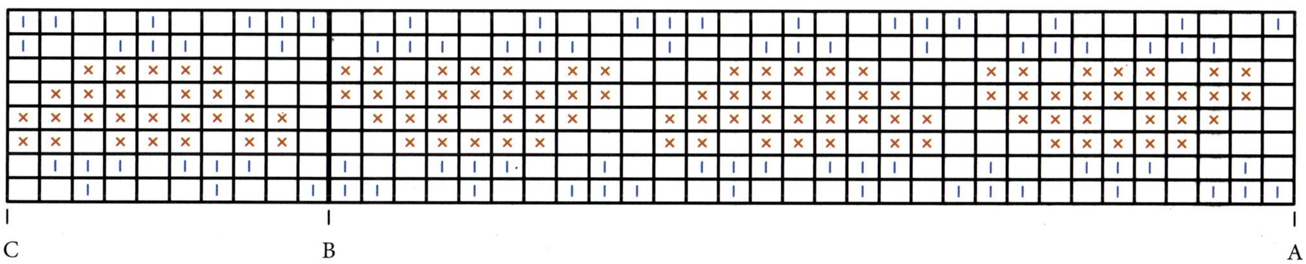

Chart B

On **right** side rows, work from A to {B-B}{C-C-C}.

On **wrong** side rows, work from {B-B}{C-C-C} to A.

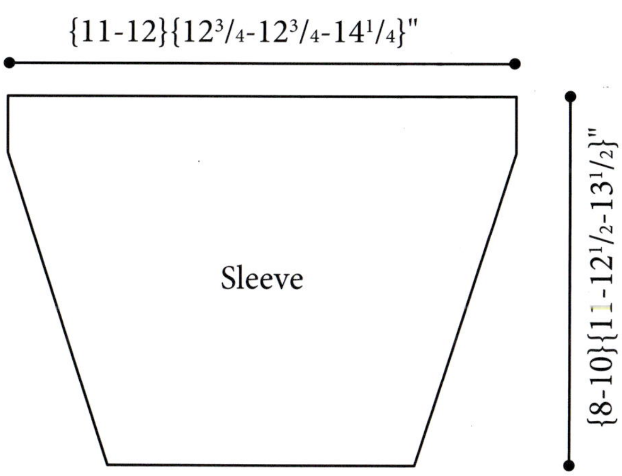

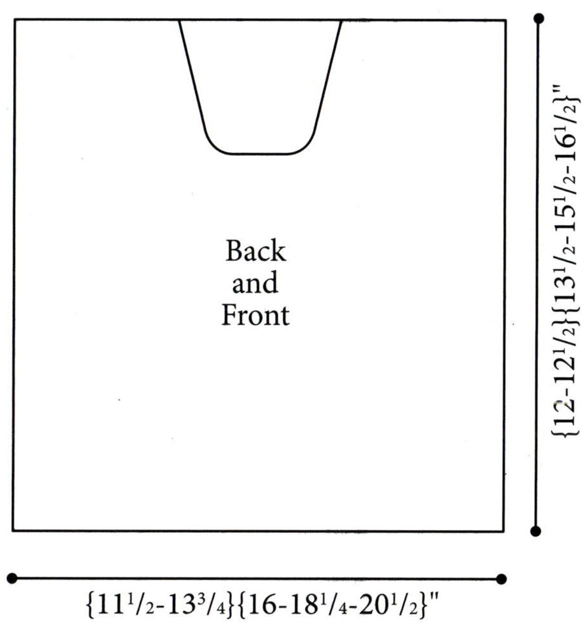

Note: Pieces include two edge stitches.

GENERAL INSTRUCTIONS

ABBREVIATIONS

cm	centimeters
K	knit
mm	millimeters
P	purl
Rnd(s)	Round(s)
SSK	slip, slip, knit
st(s)	stitch(es)
tog	together
YO	yarn over

★ — work instructions following ★ as **many more** times as indicated in addition to the first time.

( ) or [ ] — work enclosed instructions **as many** times as specified by the number immediately following **or** contains explanatory remarks.

colon (:) — the number(s) given after a colon at the end of a row or round denote(s) the number of stitches you should have on that row or round.

work even — work without increasing or decreasing in the established pattern.

GAUGE

Exact gauge is **essential** for proper size. Before beginning your project, make a sample swatch in the yarn and needle specified. After completing the swatch, measure it, counting your stitches and rows carefully. If your swatch is larger or smaller than specified, **make another, changing needle size to get the correct gauge.** Keep trying until you find the size needles that will give you the specified gauge. Once proper gauge is obtained, measure width of piece approximately every 3" (7.5 cm) to be sure gauge remains consistent.
If you have more rows per inch than specified, use a larger size needle for the purl rows; if fewer, use a smaller size needle for the purl rows.

MARKERS

As a convenience to you, we have used markers to help distinguish the beginning of a round. Place markers as instructed. You may use purchased markers or tie a length of contrasting color yarn around the needle. When you reach a marker on each round, slip it from the left needle to the right needle; remove it when no longer needed.

KNIT TERMINOLOGY		
UNITED STATES		INTERNATIONAL
gauge	=	tension
bind off	=	cast off
yarn over (YO)	=	yarn forward (yfwd) **or** yarn around needle (yrn)

KNITTING NEEDLES																
U.S.	0	1	2	3	4	5	6	7	8	9	10	10½	11	13	15	17
U.K.	13	12	11	10	9	8	7	6	5	4	3	2	1	00	000	---
Metric - mm	2	2.25	2.75	3.25	3.5	3.75	4	4.5	5	5.5	6	6.5	8	9	10	12.75

BEGINNER	Projects for first-time knitters using basic knit and purl stitches. Minimal shaping.
EASY	Projects using basic stitches, repetitive stitch patterns, simple color changes, and simple shaping and finishing.
INTERMEDIATE	Projects with a variety of stitches, such as basic cables and lace, simple intarsia, double-pointed needles and knitting in the round needle techniques, mid-level shaping and finishing.
EXPERIENCED	Projects using advanced techniques and stitches, such as short rows, fair isle, more intricate intarsia, cables, lace patterns, and numerous color changes.

ZEROS

To consolidate the length of an involved pattern, zeros are sometimes used so that all sizes can be combined. For example, increase every sixth row 5{1-0} time(s) means the first size would increase 5 times, the second size would increase once, and the largest size would do nothing.

USING COLORS

CHANGING COLORS

When changing colors, always pick up the new color of yarn from **beneath** the dropped yarn and keep the color which has just been worked to the left *(Fig. 1)*. This will prevent holes in the finished piece. Take extra care to keep your tension even.

Fig. 1

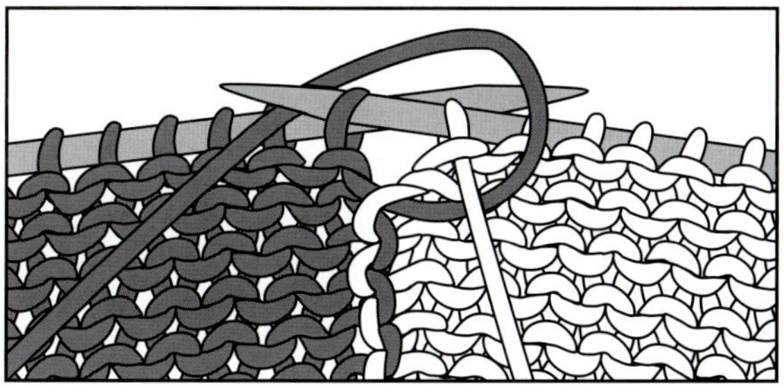

BOBBIN KNITTING

Bobbins are used to hold the small amount of yarn needed to work each color change and also to help keep the different color yarns from tangling. You'll need to wind a bobbin for each color change, using as many bobbins as necessary to avoid carrying the yarn across the back, except when there are so few stitches of the next color it would be easier to carry the unused color loosely across the back *(Fig. 2)*.

Fig. 2

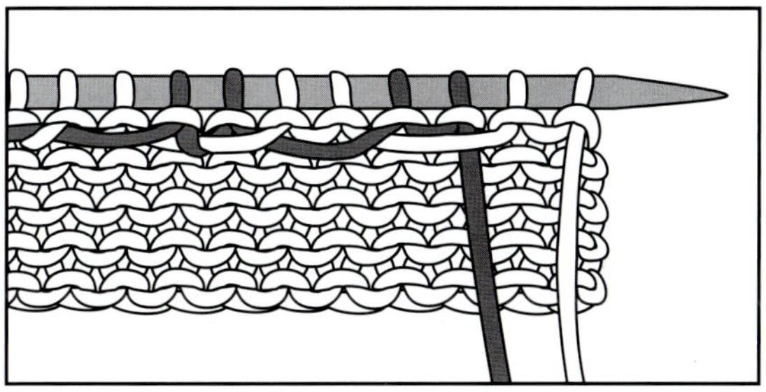

Start each bobbin as you would a new ball of yarn, leaving a 6" (15 cm) end to weave in later. Always keep the bobbins on the wrong side of your work and only unfasten enough yarn to work the area comfortably, otherwise the yarn will tangle.

Yarn Weight Symbol & Names	LACE 0	SUPER FINE 1	FINE 2	LIGHT 3	MEDIUM 4	BULKY 5	SUPER BULKY 6
Type of Yarns in Category	Fingering, size 10 crochet thread	Sock, Fingering, Baby	Sport, Baby	DK, Light Worsted	Worsted, Afghan, Aran	Chunky, Craft, Rug	Bulky, Roving
Knit Gauge Range* in Stockinette St to 4" (10 cm)	33-40** sts	27-32 sts	23-26 sts	21-24 sts	16-20 sts	12-15 sts	6-11 sts
Advised Needle Size Range	000-1	1 to 3	3 to 5	5 to 7	7 to 9	9 to 11	11 and larger

*GUIDELINES ONLY: The chart above reflects the most commonly used gauges and needle sizes for specific yarn categories.

** Lace weight yarns are usually knitted on larger needles to create lacy openwork patterns. Accordingly, a gauge range is difficult to determine. Always follow the gauge stated in your pattern.

INCREASES

KNIT INCREASE

Knit the next stitch but do **not** slip the old stitch off the left needle *(Fig. 3a)*. Insert the right needle into the **back** loop of the **same** stitch and knit it *(Fig. 3b)*, then slip the old stitch off the left needle.

Fig. 3a

Fig. 3b

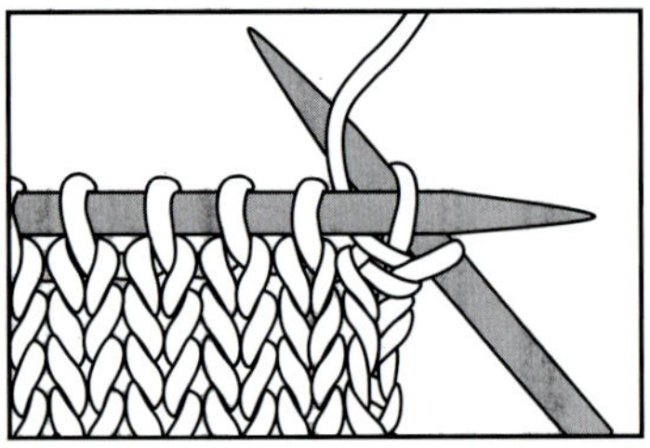

PURL INCREASE

Purl the next stitch **but do not** slip the old stitch off the left needle. Insert the right needle into the **back** loop of the **same** stitch from **back** to **front** *(Fig. 4)* and purl it. Slip the old stitch off the left needle.

Fig. 4

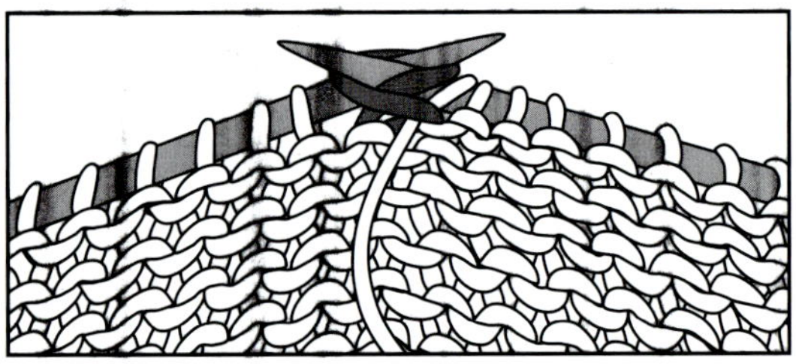

ADDING NEW STITCHES

Insert the right needle into stitch as if to **knit**, yarn over and pull loop through *(Fig. 5a)*, insert the left needle into the loop just worked from **front** to **back** and slip the loop onto the left needle *(Fig. 5b)*. Repeat for required number of stitches.

Fig. 5a

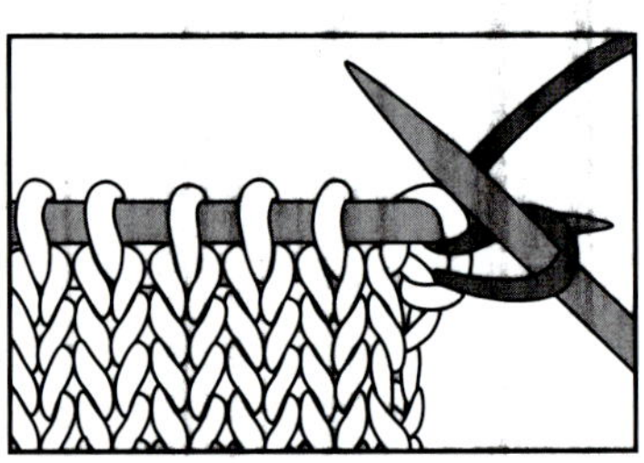

Fig. 5b

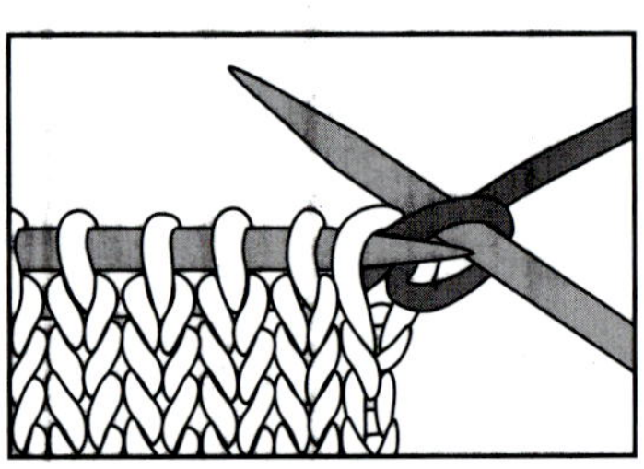

YARN OVERS *(abbreviated YO)*

After a knit stitch and before a knit stitch

Bring the yarn forward **between** the needles, then back **over** the top of the right hand needle, so that it is now in position to knit the next stitch *(Fig. 6a)*.

Fig. 6a

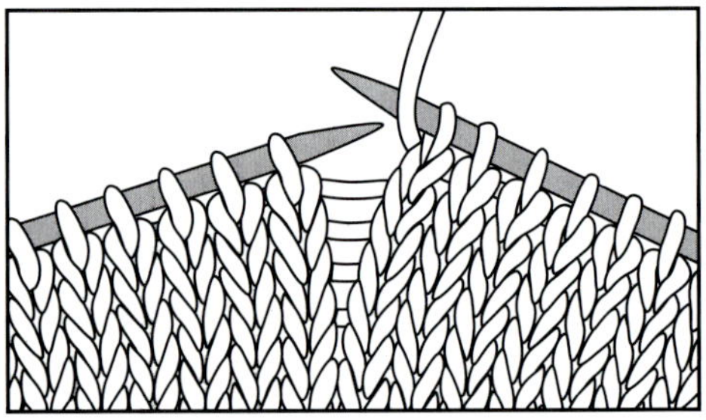

After a purl stitch and before a knit stitch

Take the yarn over the right hand needle to the back so that it is now in position to knit the next stitch *(Fig. 6b)*.

Fig. 6b

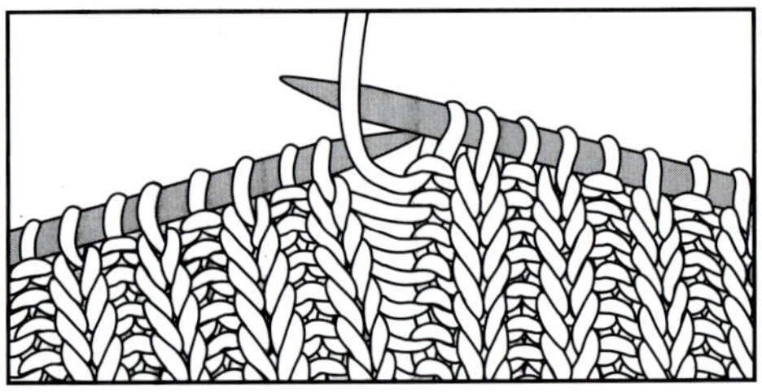

DECREASES

KNIT 2 TOGETHER *(abbreviated K2 tog)*

Insert the right needle into the **front** of the first two stitches on the left needle as if to **knit** *(Fig. 7)*, then **knit** them together as if they were one stitch.

Fig. 7

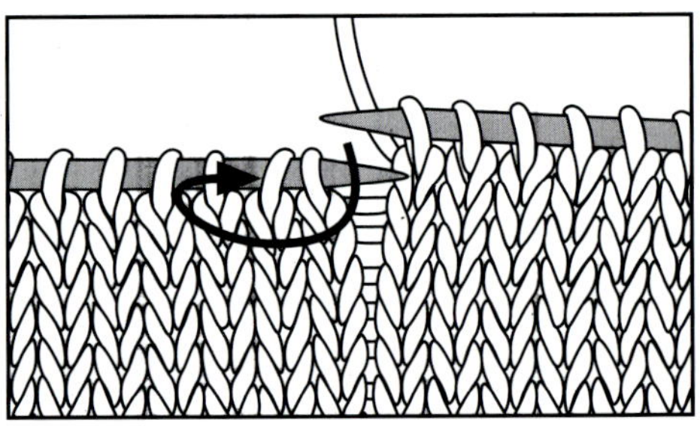

SLIP, SLIP, KNIT *(abbreviated SSK)*
Separately slip two stitches as if to **knit** *(Fig. 8a)*. Insert the left needle into the **front** of both slipped stitches *(Fig. 8b)* and knit them together as if they were one stitch *(Fig. 8c)*.

Fig. 8a

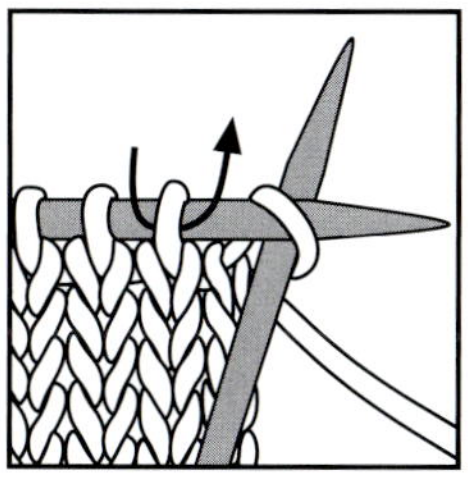

Fig. 8b

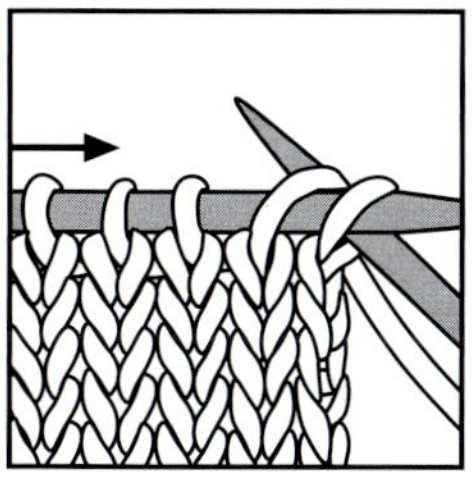

Fig. 8c

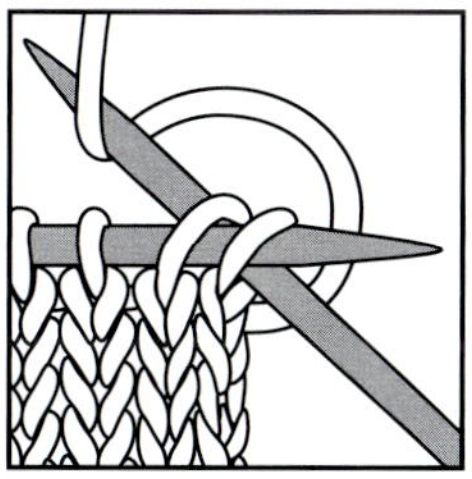

PURL 2 TOGETHER *(abbreviated P2 tog)*
Insert the right needle into the **front** of the first two stitches on the left needle as if to **purl** *(Fig. 9)*, then **purl** them together as if they were one stitch.

Fig. 9

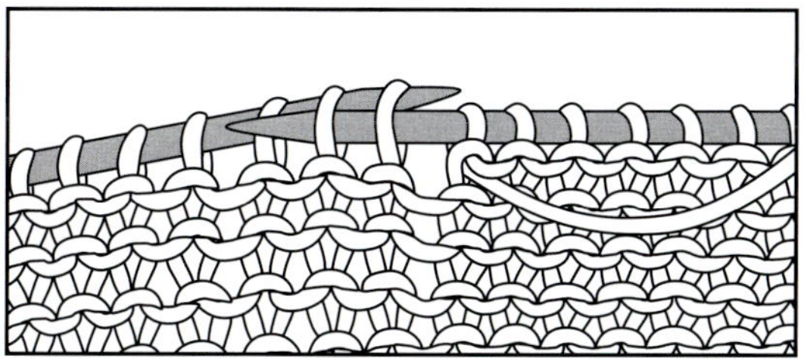

3-NEEDLE BIND OFF

Holding pieces with **right** sides together and needles parallel to each other, insert a third needle as if to **knit** into the first stitch on the front needle **and** into the first stitch on the back needle *(Fig. 10)*. Knit these two stitches together and slip them off the needle. ★ Knit the next stitch on each needle together and slip them off the needle. To bind off, insert the left needle into the first stitch on the right needle and pull the first stitch over the second stitch and off the right needle; repeat from ★ across until all of the stitches on the front needle have been bound off.

Fig. 10

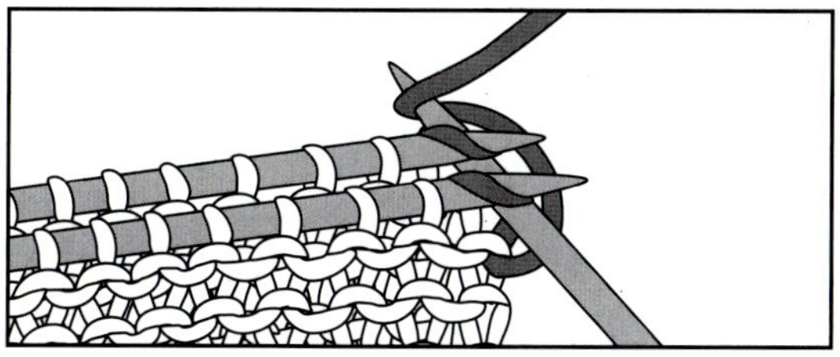

PICKING UP STITCHES

When instructed to pick up stitches, insert the needle from the **front** to the **back** under two strands at the edge of the worked piece *(Fig. 11)*. Put the yarn around the needle as if to **knit**, then bring the needle with the yarn back through the stitch to the right side, resulting in a stitch on the needle.
Repeat this along the edge, picking up the required number of stitches.
A crochet hook may be helpful to pull yarn through.

Fig. 11

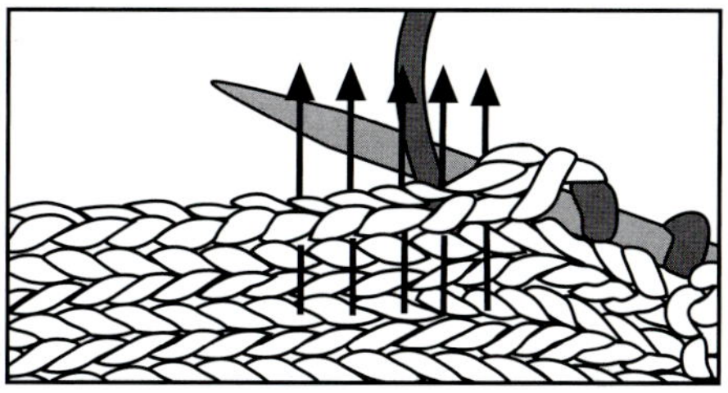

WEAVING SEAMS

With the **right** side of both pieces facing you and edges even, sew through both sides once to secure the seam. Insert the needle under the bar **between** the first and second stitches on the row and pull the yarn through *(Fig. 12)*. Insert the needle under the next bar on the second side. Repeat from side to side, being careful to match rows. If the edges are different lengths, it may be necessary to insert the needle under two bars at one edge.

Fig. 12

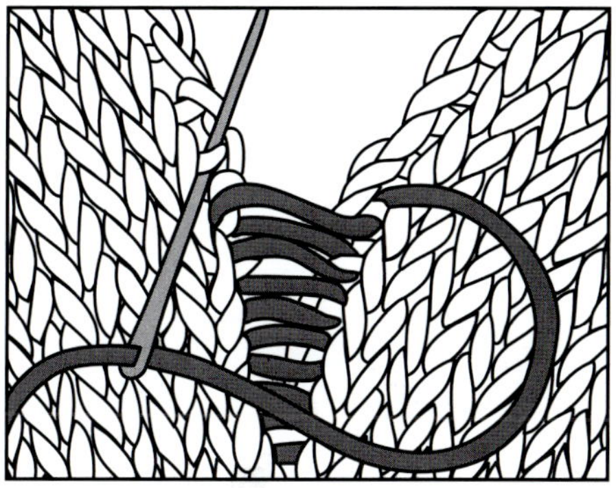

YARN INFORMATION

Each project in this leaflet was made with various weights of yarn. Any brand of yarn may be used. It is best to refer to the yardage/meters when determining how many balls or skeins to purchase. Remember, to arrive at the finished size, it is the GAUGE/TENSION that is important, not the brand of yarn.

For your convenience, listed below are the specific yarns used to create our photography models.

SCALLOPED CARDIGAN
Wendy Peter Pan Velvet Touch
#1211 Lilac Random

STRIPED PULLOVER
Cascade 220 Wool
Light Pink - #4192
Bouton D'Or Arpege
Pink - #118 Shellfish
Trendsetter Montage
Variegated - #1141 Pastel Pleasure
Note: We regret any inconvenience, but this yarn has been discontinued.

TWISTED TRIM CARDIGAN
Cascade Sierra
Pink - #16
Berroco® Cotton Twist™ Vareigated
Variegated - #8484 Uncle John's Band
Note: We regret any inconvenience, but this color has been discontinued.

EYELET CARDIGAN
Cascade Sierra
Green - #48
Blue - #22

RUFFLED PULLOVER
Cascade 220 Wool
Fuchsia - #7802
Anny Blatt N°5
Light Blue - #215
Tahki Jolie
Pink - #5004 Light Pink
Europa Peacock
Variegated - #01
Note: We regret any inconvenience, but this yarn has been discontinued.

Production Team: Instructional Editor - Sarah J. Green; Technical Editor - Joan Beebe; Editorial Writer - Susan McManus Johnson; Graphic Artist - Dayle Carozza; Senior Graphic Artist - Lora Puls; Photo Stylist - Cassie Francioni; and Photographer - Jason Masters.